Dear Reader,

We all need our own little BLUEPRINTS, or plans, in life. Sometimes making a plan is fun. Sometimes it's hard. Sometimes the plan doesn't work, so we make a new one. And sometimes, the plan is exactly what we need, just when we need it. As you read this Have a Plan Book, we hope you will ask questions, talk about it with family and friends, and create your very own plan. You can do this on your own or together with a grown-up.

Your plan may grow and change each time you read your book, and that's great! As life happens, plans change. But remember, having a little Blueprint is always helpful, in difficult times and in good times. So go ahead: BLUEPRINT IT!

Lovingly,

Your friends at little BLUEPRINT

P.S. Children and adults around the world are making their own little BLUEPRINTS. If you want to see the plans of others, or share yours, just go to

www.littleBLUEPRINT.com

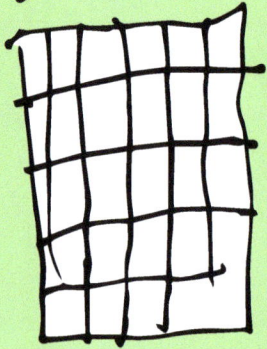

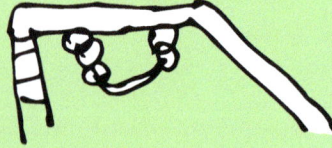

a partment

playground

book store

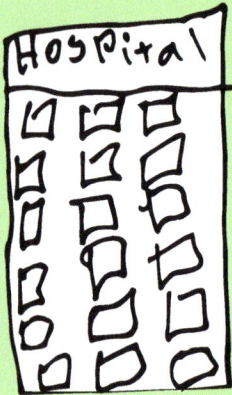

Hospital

HAVE A PLAN *Books*

To purchase a hardcover or
personalized version of any
little BLUEPRINT book,
with names, optional photo(s),
and details, please go to:

www.littleBLUEPRINT.com

bont

toy store

The author would like to thank,
for all of their support and expertise:
Dan Siegel, M.D.;
Nina Shapiro, M.D.;
Pattie Fitzgerald
(Founder, Safely Ever After, Inc., www.safelyeverafter.com);
my editors, Leslie Budnick and Gina Shaw.
A special thanks to:
Vicente Foods, Los Angeles, California;
Phoebe, age 10, for her blueprint illustration; and
Noa Paige, age 7, for her title page illustration.

Play ground

Hons

House

bont

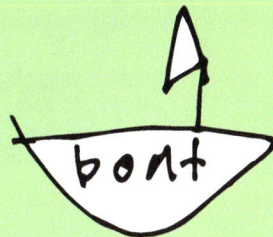

toy store

TO BE SAFE
on the Go,
I HAVE A PLAN

by Katherine Eskovitz

illustrated by Jessica Churchill

a partment

Hospital

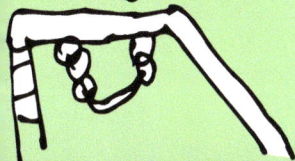

playground

book store

I am safe when I am on the go.

I LOVE GOING PLACES . . .

exploring a park with friends,

choosing my favorite topping at the yogurt store,

and searching for the perfect book at the library.

Being **SAFE** means that I am not in danger,
and I do not get hurt.
I stay safe because my parents and others teach me to be safe.

SAFE ADULTS are people my parents and I trust. They do not make me uncomfortable, and they always follow **SAFETY RULES** to help keep me safe.

I can stay safe on the go just by following
some simple safety rules at a park, store,
or any place where there are lots of people.

If I am at a fair, and I'm going on a ride, or trying to win a big stuffed animal, it is smart to make sure I can always see the SAFE ADULT I came with.

If I wander off too far, my safe adult may not be able to see me.

BE SAFE: STAY NEAR MY SAFE ADULT WHEN ON THE GO.

If I think I am lost,

I should **STOP** right where I am so I don't get too far away. Then, I **YELL** for my safe adult. I do not wander away because it will be harder for my safe adult to find me.

IF I AM LOST, it is really smart to ask a **MOM WITH KIDS** for help.

She can understand how I feel and can help me find my way.

If I cannot find a mom with kids,
and I am LOST IN A STORE,
I can go to a CASHIER, where we pay, to ask for help.

IF I GET LOST OUTSIDE, and I cannot find a mom with kids, I can look for a person in uniform, such as a POLICE OFFICER, to help me. But I should never get into a car with anyone, even if they seem nice. A safe adult will never ask me to leave when I am lost.

BE SAFE: ASK FOR HELP FIRST FROM A MOM WITH KIDS; SECOND, A CASHIER; AND THIRD, A POLICE OFFICER. I NEVER GET IN A CAR WITH ANYONE WHEN I AM LOST.

I can memorize my parents'
NAMES, ADDRESS, and PHONE NUMBER(S).

NAMES:

_____

_____

ADDRESS:

_____

_____

PHONE NUMBER(S):

_____

_____

That way, if I get lost or need help, I have all the
information I need for someone to help me,
and I can reach my parents wherever they are...

BE SAFE: ALWAYS KNOW MY PARENTS' CONTACT INFORMATION.

I know NEVER, NEVER, NEVER to leave a park, a store, or wherever I am without my parents or my safe adult…

EVEN for just a minute,

EVEN if someone offers to give me a present or a treat,

EVEN if someone knows my name,

I never leave without my safe adult.

EVEN if someone tells me that my parents said it is OK to leave,

EVEN if someone says they need my help,

EVEN if someone is really, really nice to me,

I never leave without my safe adult.

People may be very sweet to me, but they are **NOT** safe adults if they do not follow SAFETY RULES.

A SAFE ADULT knows that it is my job to **CHECK FIRST** before going anywhere with anyone.

BE SAFE: ALWAYS CHECK FIRST WITH MY SAFE ADULT BEFORE GOING ANYWHERE WITH ANYONE.

In addition to following safety rules,

we each have our very own safety protector inside of us.

We have feelings that we can listen to
and trust to keep us safe.

These feelings are called our

INTUITION.

My INTUITION tells me if I am

SCARED, UNSURE, OR UNCOMFORTABLE.

My head or stomach might hurt, my heart might beat faster,

or it might be hard for me to breathe.

I might tell myself that something seems odd or wrong.

The safety protector inside of me is sending me a clue

that there might be DANGER.

My intuition is very smart.

I should always pay attention to these clues because my feelings can protect me from danger.

If my INTUITION tells me something is not quite right

—I FEEL IT QUIETLY INSIDE OF ME—

I SHOULD ALWAYS TRUST THIS FEELING.

BE SAFE: LISTEN TO MY INTUTION TO HELP KEEP ME SAFE.

One of the most important things about going out is that I can have fun and still stay safe as long as *I follow the safety rules.*

My Plan
1. Practice and memorize cell phone number.
2. Always check first with a safe adult.
3. Trust my INTUITION if I think something is wrong.

4.

5.

I can help to stay safe when I'm on the go by creating my own SAFETY PLAN, together with my family.

SAMPLE PLAN

1. BE SAFE: STAY NEAR MY SAFE ADULT WHEN ON THE GO.

2. BE SAFE: STOP AND YELL IF I THINK I AM LOST.

3. BE SAFE: ASK FOR HELP FIRST FROM A MOM WITH KIDS;
   SECOND, A CASHIER; AND THIRD, A POLICE OFFICER.
   I NEVER GET IN A CAR WITH ANYONE WHEN I AM LOST.

4. BE SAFE: ALWAYS KNOW MY PARENTS' CONTACT INFORMATION.

5. BE SAFE: ALWAYS CHECK FIRST WITH MY SAFE ADULT
   BEFORE GOING ANYWHERE WITH ANYONE.

6. BE SAFE: LISTEN TO MY INTUTION TO HELP KEEP ME SAFE.

Here is MY PLAN

Check out other children's BLUEPRINTS from around the world and share yours, too!

Other titles in the
HAVE A PLAN Series

TO BE A HEALTHY EATER, I HAVE A PLAN

TO CELEBRATE THE HOLIDAYS, I HAVE A PLAN

WHEN I MISS SOMEONE SPECIAL, I HAVE A PLAN

WHEN I MISS MY SPECIAL PET, I HAVE A PLAN

TO BE SAFE AT HOME, I HAVE A PLAN

WHEN IT'S TIME FOR BED, I HAVE A PLAN

TO KEEP MY BODY SAFE, I HAVE A PLAN

WHEN MY PARENTS DIVORCE, I HAVE A PLAN

WHEN MY PARENTS SEPARATE, I HAVE A PLAN

AND MORE

New titles added regularly at

www.littleBLUEPRINT.com

All titles are available ready-made and personalized

www.ingramcontent.com/pod-product-compliance
Lightning Source LLC
LaVergne TN
LVHW072101070426

835508LV00002B/211